Hounding the Hun from the Seas

A Tale of the British M. L.'s
on the High Seas

By

LIEUTENANT M—P—S
(R.N.V.R.)

With notes from and gratitude

to

LIEUTENANT E. P. DAWSON'S
(R.N.V.R.)

book "PUSHING WATER"
JOHN LANE COMPANY

London Graphic Pictures © Underwood & Underwood, N. Y.

Copyright 1919
THE ELCO WORKS
of
ELECTRIC BOAT COMPANY
BAYONNE, NEW JERSEY, U. S. A.

Manufacturers of
Motor Yachts   Motor Boats
Yacht Tenders   Gasoline Engines
Electric Launches

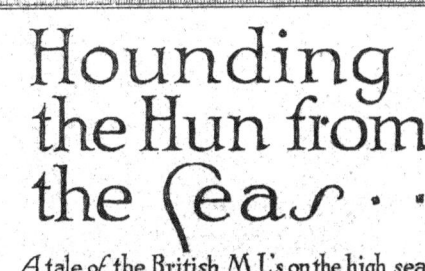

Hounding the Hun from the Seas..

A tale of the British M.L.'s on the high seas

Salvaging the remains of a Boche aeroplane just brought down by an M. L. anti-aircraft gun.

THE for'ard 3-inch gun swung to port, sighted for one thousand yards—and let go. On our port bow a great U-boat lay to, quietly charging her storage batteries. She was well up, the conning tower a good eight feet above the lazy swell—she lay, a pretty target, in the half light that precedes the dawn off the North coast of Scotland.

Sharp orders flashed and our little 80-foot Submarine Chaser slewed around and made for the pirate—full speed ahead, firing as she went.

It was the moment for which we had all been waiting. We had received a wireless that a big U-boat was operating off the Scottish coast; but for three days we had sighted nothing save a drifting mine, which we exploded with a well-placed rifle shot. And now, here was our quarry in full sight, unprepared, wallowing like a huge whale.

At our first shot she got under way, her periscope disappearing beneath the surface before we could cover half the distance that separated us.

Anxious moments followed; then suddenly, from our cockney cook, came the excited cry:

"Lor' blimey—there she be naow—'ow abart it?"

The U-boat had changed her course, and broached on our starboard bow. Something was wrong with her gear, or she would have remained submerged and taken a chance with our depth bombs.

Swiftly we swung around and were pounding at her again. But she submerged a second time—to reappear inside of two minutes.

Our 3-incher barked again, making our little ship tremble from top to keel. Then came a wild shout from all of us. It was a direct hit! We had struck her in the magazine and the explosion that followed was terrific. She rose, bow first, in a burst of flame, almost entirely clear of the water—and then disappeared in a fountain of oily spray.

"Thet's th' finish o' thet blighter. But"—groused our cockney cook, "lahk es nawt, we'll never find naw-

"It was a direct hit."

think to tike 'ome—nawthink but bubbles an' a lot o' bloomin' oil—nawt so much es a packet o' fags, or a Fritzie cap."

But he was wrong this time, for as we came over the spot where the U-boat had sunk we cut our way through thick oil and floating debris. This, together with the snapshots we had taken at the moment of the explosion, would be ample proof for the most exacting Board of the British Admiralty—which demands complete verification before it will give credit for the sinking of a U-boat.

But the British Admiralty is strict in everything. I remember their demands of the American shipbuilders—who had built the very craft I was on—demands as to stability, speed, cruising radius and a host of other stiff construction requirements, before they would even take an interest in the plan of the American concern for fighting Submarines with a fleet of fast Motor Launches.

Our cockney cook put it more warmly:

"W'en th' ol' geezers awsked th' Yanks t' build these 'ere crawfts—they were awskin' them t' fetch a lump o' ice through 'ell. An' strike me pink—they nawt only did it—but mide rawsberry sherbet on the wy!"

And that is just about what happened.

The story of how one of the foremost boat-building concerns in the United States finally convinced the British Admiralty that Yankee ingenuity could surmount almost insuperable difficulties—and then proved it by building 550 Submarine Chasers in 488 days, or more than a boat a day—is a monument to the ability and efficiency of American methods for all time. It is a record I am particularly proud of, in that I had some part in the making of it.

In the early summer of 1914 I had crossed to America to put the finishing touches to an education in marine technology—before taking my place in my father's shipyard on the Clyde.

Through a friend I was persuaded to spend a few

A fleet of "Movies" rushing to capture a German "sub" just bombed by a "blimp."

months in the draughting-room of what he told me was the most progressive boat-building company in America.

I was there, in The Elco Works at Bayonne, New Jersey, when the Great War broke out in August of 1914 —and was just preparing to return to England, when a German U-boat torpedoed and sunk three British cruisers, the "Aboukir," the "Cressy" and the "Hogue"— all within a few hours—and threw the British Admiralty into a panic. How was England to kill off this German menace that was threatening the complete destruction of her shipping?

England immediately despatched a high Admiralty officer to investigate the Yankee plan—with orders to report without delay.

Our plan was to build quickly a fleet of fifty Motor Launches large enough to operate in the treacherous weather of the North Sea; capable of a 19-knot speed, in service trim, and with a cruising radius of one thousand miles. They were to be equipped with heavy duty gasoline motors, afford accommodations for two officers and seven men—and mount a 3-inch gun. Though they must be able to weather any sea—they had to be small enough to be conveniently sent abroad on the decks of British transports—limiting their over-all length to 80 feet.

"It can't be done!" cabled the British Admiralty to The Elco Works.

"Give us the chance and we'll show you," we cabled back.

An M. L. and a "blimp" exchanging information.

On April 9th, 1915, they gave us the first order for fifty boats, and by the first of May we had the "master" or pattern boat in frame.

A week later the "Lusitania" was sunk.

When the appalling news came, we were giving the British Admiralty's representative a farewell dinner at Delmonico's. He was much depressed, and, before saying good-bye, asked whether we thought we could take care of a much larger order. It was then that we guaranteed to build a boat a day, as long as the Admiralty would need them . . . As soon as he reached England we received a cablegram ordering five hundred additional "M. L.'s."

It was a twenty-two million dollar contract, and when some of the biggest bankers in the United States were asked by England to finance the project they said the plan was preposterous.

"How," they asked, "can a plant, which has built perhaps a dozen yachts and twenty or thirty smaller craft a year, produce a Submarine Chaser a day, which will fulfill the tremendously difficult requirements of the British Admiralty?"

"Our standardization will do it," obstinately held the head of the Elco. "Gentlemen, if you won't help, we'll have to do it alone."

And "do it alone" we did.

Those were mighty exciting days. England's outlook

was gray and fast getting black. Across her horizon there sprawled the apparition of a monstrous U-boat—a fearful thing, threatening to seize and drown all human beings upon the seas. These American-built Submarine Chasers seemed a forlorn hope to her.

And it was under these pessimistic foreboding conditions that we undertook to "carry th' lump o' ice through 'ell."

The United States had not yet declared war on Germany, and the very delicate question of neutrality had to be handled with utmost discretion; so the first lot was built and completed in Bayonne; camouflaged as private yachts, and slipped away in the night to Canada, a journey of a thousand miles. There they were lifted aboard waiting transports and sent to England.

But it was clear that we couldn't assemble the remaining five hundred "M. L.'s" in Bayonne, and equally clear that Canada offered a convenient field of operation —so I was sent up to report on a small "repair yard" opposite Quebec.

What we could get of this yard was little more than a

Every passing ship must be challenged, stopped and examined.

"rock pile" and a cow pasture, fronting on a sullen river, which, even as late as April, is filled with drifting ice.

Very good for cows—but very poor for boats. However, we took it over and added another yard at Montreal.

We planned to build every individual part of the boats in Bayonne; keel, frames, planking, interior woodwork, plumbing, piping and fittings—all of which was to be shipped to our Canadian plants, with the two main engines, made by the Standard engine people—each capable of developing 225 H.P. All these fabricated parts were to be assembled into complete boats at Montreal and Quebec and then transported to England.

By that time I had become fairly familiar with the work at Bayonne and my company sent me to Quebec to help organize operations there.

In Quebec I found that all of the workmen were rough Canadian backwoodsmen, most of whom had never seen a motor boat before.

These men were to build our snow and cold-proof sheds, as the average snowfall there is from fifteen to eighteen feet, with the temperature frequently forty degrees below zero—and then to accomplish the delicate work of assembly—for the Elco "M. L.'s," while highly tuned, had to be thoroughly staunch and seaworthy.

I was about completely staggered the first day, when all the terrific odds we were working against seemed to march before me at once—one of them being that practically none of the Canucks spoke English. But I had brought up North with me twenty of the best workmen from Bayonne; sturdy, resourceful Americans, capable of meeting any situation that might arise. With these for the nucleus of our small army, we were all soon plunged into a maelstrom of hard work, and in remarkably short time we had big serviceable buildings erected and were beginning the work of assembly.

For years The Elco Company had been working upon the theory of a thorough *standardization* of boats—just as the manufacture of an automobile, a sewing machine or a McCormick harvester is *standardized*. And now the opportunity had come to prove the theory on a big scale.

Each separate and individual part, from the keel to the little truck at the masthead, was designed, tried out, changed and changed again, until it fitted perfectly. It was then detailed and given a symbol, indicating where, and in what particular boat, it was to go.

Our Canadian workmen were divided into small groups, each group assigned to a definite operation. The boat parts would come up to us all labeled, so that assembling

them was much like the working out of a jig-saw puzzle. A "master key" or chart was kept at Bayonne, with each step of our progress constantly checked up. In that way our work was completely standardized.

An intense spirit of great rush pervaded us, body and soul. It was a race against death and the submarine. Every man understood the significance of that race and every man worked with a grim determination to win.

Shortly after the first fifty "M. L.'s" reached English waters, Winter closed in upon us and blocked the possibility of further deliveries at Quebec or Montreal until Spring.

That meant months of idleness, while trans-Atlantic shipping was being destroyed.

We determined to overcome this obstacle by shipping the "M. L.'s" by rail to Halifax. This necessitated sending 80-foot boats on 60-foot Northwest lumber cars. We accomplished it with trailers to take care of the overhang, and by Christmas, 1915, we were shipping eight or nine boats a week, and had settled down to the more or less monotonous routine of standardized production in great quantity.

But frequently the "monotony" was broken by our discovery of bomb plots and by our catching German spies. These same spies threatened all of our plants— and but for the eternal alertness of our military guards would likely have succeeded in destroying them.

At Halifax the boats were launched and put through

rigorous trials—for each boat had to be inspected and passed by the British Overseers, before it could be shipped abroad—*and not one boat ever failed to fulfill every requirement.*

But the British Admiralty, unused to fast Motor Launches, were "grousing"—and so it was decided to send our chief engineer across to show them how to handle our "M.L.'s." And as the work in our Canadian plants was now so efficiently organized as to operate almost automatically—it was decided that I be sent across with him.

M. L.'s aboard a transport driving off a submarine.

We shipped on a transport carrying four "M. L.'s" lashed to the deck—and had a fairly uneventful voyage, until the day we first saw the Irish coast—when at 2 P. M. we sighted the periscope of a U-boat.

She evidently knew our transport was unarmed, for she quickly came to the surface and began shelling us. Save for our desperate zig-zagging, we were helpless.

Then I thought of the 3-inch guns aboard the "M.L.'s." We tore off the tarpaulins and got them into action, putting up a running fight with the "sub."

How I ached to have just one of those "M. L.'s" in the water to go after that "Sea Sneak," instead of being helpless aboard ship. We'd have made short work of her! As it was, we fought her off for a full three hours, under the most difficult conditions.

Then a blessed fog enveloped us and we slipped away to safety and the shores of England.

But when we arrived in England there was another difficult task confronting us—that of silencing the constitutional habit of "grousing" on the part of the Britishers.

They were skeptical about everything concerning American-built craft. The British Admiral of one port said he thought such "little fellows" would be sure to "turn turtle," once in the trough in a Channel storm.

But, when a bad storm did descend on the Channel, we asked him if he would come aboard with us for a

The "Movie" is "like a drunken streak of lightning."

demonstration. He looked dubiously at the sky and sea —but was game. So we stepped aboard a newly arrived "M. L." and headed out into the teeth of the gale.

It was a rough trip. We'd slide with sickening speed from the top of a mountainous wave down into the trough, only to ride up on the next and repeat the performance endlessly.

An "M. L.'s" movement is more like a drunken streak of lightning than anything else.

Then we let the helm go altogether, leaving the "little-un" to shift for herself. It was an anxious moment and we half expected the first towering wave would engulf us. But she rode it like a thoroughbred.

The Admiral was thoroughly convinced of our craft's

ability to stand up in any weather, and became enthusiastic over its possibilities.

One day, shortly after, when the sea was calmer, the Admiral suggested showing us the operation of a depth charge.

We were aboard one of the "School M. L.'s," out in the Solent, and going it fairly slow, when the charge was ordered dropped from the stern and the signal rung for full speed ahead.

But, in the excitement to get away—the green engineer became rattled—and *stalled his engines.*

There we were, slowly drifting, with a depth charge holding enough T N T to blow a score of boats like ours out of the sea, due to explode in a few seconds.

Of all the exciting experiences I had later, while on active duty aboard an "M. L.," I believe that was the most *interesting.* We had barely cleared the depth charge by two hundred feet when it exploded, spouting a great geyser astern, tossing our craft like a cork and nearly smothering us with spray.

* * * *

After we had thoroughly demonstrated the value of our "M. L.'s," the Admiralty began taking them seriously and established training schools for engineers and crews—recruited chiefly from yachtsmen of England.

I was anxious to get into active duty myself, as the difficulties in building the boats no longer held so strong a claim upon me. So I enlisted as a lieutenant in the R. N. V. R.; and, after completing my training, was ordered to active duty.

I was assigned to an "M. L." at a North Sea Base in Scotland, and had barely time to get my gear together

Signaling a big steamer to lay-to.

before we were ordered to sea, and proceeded to our station, sixty miles off Peterhead.

We were officially known as the Auxiliary Motor Boat Patrol. But when you describe the "M. L." itself, you have a varied choice of names to choose from, but the name we like best ourselves is the "Movies." There is something about the name "Movie" which seems to fit; for an "M. L." is nothing if not movement.

Our particular "pigeon" was to patrol. Every passing ship must be challenged, stopped and examined—she may be another "Moewe" or some "Hunnish" neutral, willing to run any risk for the sake of Hun gold.

There were sometimes most exciting chases.

A big steamer would be thinking more about submarines than "Movies," so, when we Morsed her to stop, the skipper usually got a bad attack of nerves—concluded we were a "sub"—and rang for full speed ahead.

Then would come as glorious a race as ever seen at a

Chivying a "big one" into port.

regatta—the big ship forging ahead, at top speed and possibly zig-zagging, while the insignificant "Movie" whoops along astern, one mass of spray, but always gaining.

There was always the chance of the big fellow using his gun—and I have seen him do it—but it was up to us to convince him of our friendly intentions. When finally convinced, the big ship would stop and we would go alongside, step aboard and express our apologies. If everything was O. K. we'd wish him *bon-voyage* and give him "sailing orders." If not—we'd rattle our revolvers, to make him realize that the whole British

The Cruisers "Intrepid," "Iphigenia" and "Thetis," surrounded by "Movies," entering the harbor preparatory to sinking them in the Channel.

April 22, 1918

The "Vindictive" laid alongside the Mole.

Navy was behind us, and send him into the nearest port for further examination.

If ever you have seen a small terrier at the heels of a dray-horse, you have some idea of the ludicrous appearance of a "Movie" chivying a 6,000-ton freighter into an examination port.

* * * *

The weather off the Scottish coast is tricky and usually downright nasty. Terrific storms seem suddenly to blow up from nowhere, blacken the sky and howl and rage over the sea, challenging the lives of every one. It was off this coast and in such a storm that the great Lord Kitchener was lost.

Added to this was the extreme cold. We went on deck

The "brooms" of the Grand Fleet.

in "duffels"—thick blanket-cloth coats with hoods like Alaskan parkas. I had been up in the Arctic and thought I knew what cold was, but never have I known such damp, penetrating, keen cold as we experienced when patrolling off the Scottish coast. And then there was the problem of mess. Sometimes for days we would live on uncooked food, because the bucking, tearing sea made it impossible to hold even a pot of tea on the galley stove.

But our moments of intense excitement and danger largely made up for our physical discomforts.

There are many things about the "Movie" that can only be whispered—that is why we were among the "Hush-Hush" class of His Britannic Majesty's Navy.

We were the "eyes of that Navy"—everywhere patrolling, watching and vigilant, so that no spot around the British Isles might go unsearched—so that no patch of seaboard might be a death-trap to the merchantmen that placed food upon John Bull's breakfast table.

While our steady job was patrolling, we had many auxiliary stunts to perform. Before the Grand Fleet could sail, the "brooms" had to do their work—and we were the "brooms."

Our engines were not running all the time, for gasoline is a valuable commodity, and a "Movie" consumes gasoline with the same avidity that a flapper consumes chocolates. "Save gasoline," was the strict injunction to the C. O. of a "Movie." Hence we must do a drifting patrol. A drifting patrol means running to a certain position, then shutting off your engines and drifting with the current and wind, for hours at a time.

Almost daily we ran through the slimy trail of the U-boat. We would sight the wreckage of torpedoed ships and many times were able to rescue survivors, who had been forced to take to their small boats. In most cases their condition was pitiable. I have seen them, after eight or nine days at sea in open boats, crying for water and exhausted by fatigue and hunger—seen them bleached by the salt water, their skin eaten into and cracked by the salt—horrible sights.

Patrolling the North Sea, 60 miles off Peterhead.

Twice we picked up these drifting boats, with gaunt bodies rolling in the bilges—mute witnesses to the savagery of the Hun.

First, last and all time—however—we were looking for *Fritz*. The speed of the "Movies," the protection their miniature size afforded as a target, their waspish nature, as regards guns and explosive inventions, have proved so inimical to the U-boats that the Hun always preferred to make himself scarce in our vicinity.

It was usually in the early morning that we would come upon U-boats, afloat on the surface, recharging their batteries.

One murky morning, when a bad sea was running, we suddenly came upon a huge submarine, wallowing in the trough, but were too close upon her to use our gun—and we rang for full speed ahead, aiming to ram her just abaft the conning tower.

I ran to get a lance-bomb (a long stick, looking like a large bullrush, with a T N T bomb for the head)—and was running for'ard to hammer-throw it at the "sub"—when we struck her head on.

The force of our rush made us ride up on her deck, leaving her apparently uninjured, but smashing our bow.

It was a very ticklish situation. We all jumped for guns and pistols, watching the silent conning tower for the next move.

The "Movies" were the eyes and ea

—all the five senses of the Fleet.

Slowly it opened and a man stepped out on the deck of the submarine.

Every move he made was deliberate, unhurried—and seemed to breathe contempt—as he walked slowly over to the bow of our "M. L."—with all our eyes centered upon him intently.

Finally he turned to us, bowed—and asked, in good London English, if we wouldn't like a tow.

We had rammed an English E-boat and the man speaking to us was her skipper. I'll pass briefly over how we felt. I still had the lance-bomb in my hand, poised for a throw—and looked particularly foolish. But it is often impossible to distinguish an E-boat from a U-boat, and we couldn't afford to take chances.

Mine sweeping—to make the Seas safe.

Our for'ard bulkheads floated us and, with the aid of the submarine, we made port, where we laid up for repairs.

Now I've been telling you a lot about our duties and our "M. L.'s"—I'd like to stop for a moment to tell you of the sort of men we had to man them.

This is the tale of a sub-lieutenant who was ordered to duty on our "Movie." He was a Manchester lad, raised from the lower deck and given a commission for gallantry in action with a submarine. Besides wound stripes he wore the D. S. O.

For weeks we could not get him to tell us how he won the decoration. All he would say was, "I'm no 'ero." But finally we learned his story:

In an attack, a submarine came up so close that it was impossible to deflect the "M. L.'s" gun enough to fire into her. This little Manchester lad grabbed a rifle and coolly picked off the submarine's gun crew before they could train their own gun; and the two ships drifted apart sufficiently for his mates to get their gun into action. The submarine was destroyed—but his own "M. L." was torpedoed. "I didn't want to tell you, because I've been torpedoed twice, and I thought you might think I was a Jonah."

Such was the type of men who manned our "M. L.'s."

* * * *

In one particular locality "Movies" acted as tenders

to aeroplanes. Here our special stunt was to pick up the pilots from aeroplanes that had broken down off the enemy's coast. This meant running through German mine fields and working, almost continuously, under German batteries.

In a way our "Movies" were ideal ships for this service, as they stood a better chance than the larger ships of not "clicking" a mine—and proved very poor targets for the German batteries. But at best the work was hazardous enough.

Among our many duties was to work in conjunction with the regular mine sweepers. To do this the "Movie" was fitted with the regular gear for sweeping—and did exceptionally well, for even when towing the heavy sweep cable we covered almost twice as much ground as

One of the Fleet of 110-ft. Submarine Chasers built for the U. S. Navy.

the drifters and trawlers, while our shoal draft made us less vulnerable.

Nearly all mines—or "eggs" as we called them—are sown a few feet beneath the surface of the water and held there by anchors. Accordingly, our sweep wires are designed to stay under the surface and cut the moorings of the mines—causing them to rise to the surface, where they are exploded by rifle fire.

It is highly dangerous work and men who did this sort of thing regularly developed quite a special set of characteristics—for you never know when you may "click" a mine by disturbing one of their many protruding "horns," setting off a detonator—with disastrous results.

There is considerable sporting interest in exploding mines with rifle fire. The anchor cable must first be fouled by your sweep wire and the mine brought to the surface, either free of its anchor or dragging it. Then the trick is to hit one of the small protruding "horns" with a rifle shot. In a lively sea this takes some crack shooting. Altogether mine sweeping is a nerve-racking job—the best part of a day at it is the end of it.

One morning, following a long session at mine sweeping, we went through an odd experience. It was a gray dawn and the sea had an unhealthy quiet. Just as daylight lifted we sighted a big U-boat, lying perfectly still on the surface, about a mile away.

We were on the *qui vive* in an instant and sped toward

her, firing as we went. Several direct hits were recorded as we neared her—but the U-boat remained as still as the sea she was on—no return fire—no attempt to get away—not a sign of life about her.

When we had come within a few boat lengths of her we scored a vital hit and she sank, stern first.

"Twelve 'Movies' immediately left the harbor."

It was weird and uncanny. Whether our first shot had crippled her engines and imprisoned her crew, or whether they were already dead, we never knew. But down she went and nothing but a pool of oil, a few pieces of woodwork—yes—and a Fritzie cap—remained on the calm sea, to mark a grave for the dead.

The strangeness of men's hearts showed then. Not a shout escaped us, but instead—a dead silence. Our cockney cook was standing beside me. There was moisture in his eye and his face said "poor devils," though never a word passed his lips. Our gunner broke the spell by firing a salute across the pool of oil.

Then a smudge was sighted on the horizon and we headed to sea again.

The smudge proved to be a hospital ship that had been driven far off her course by U-boats and was now working her way down to Dover. We escorted her until we picked up another "Movie" and left her under its protection.

Everywhere in European waters our "Movies" were having similar experiences. The following incident occurred at Gibraltar, in April, 1918.

There were approximately twenty-five "Movies" at the Naval Base, at Gibraltar, when, one night, word was received that German "subs" were operating in the neighborhood.

Twelve "Movies," three torpedo boats and a drifter immediately left the harbor. They sailed in two lines, with half a mile distance between them. At about half after three in the morning the drifter sighted a strange ship and forged ahead to investigate.

Not having enough speed the drifter signaled the nearest "Movie." As the "Movie" approached the stranger she switched on her sailing lights to avoid collision. And upon seeing this, the stranger, which was in reality a German U-boat, started to submerge.

The C. O. of the "Movie" rushed aft to set the depth charges, which gave the "sub" time to submerge completely. Four charges were fired. Two to explode at a forty-foot depth and two to explode at eighty.

It was too dark then to see anything, but later, when daylight came, the water was thickly strewn with debris. Doors, with brass hinges pulled away, teakwood shell-racks, gratings and all sorts of deck gear, saturated with oil.

The battle-scarred "Vindictive."

These evidences were submitted to the British Admiralty—and M. L. 413 was credited with a German submarine.

As one of the officers remarked: "The sinking of that one U-boat, preventing the damage she would have done to Mediterranean shipping, more than paid for England's entire 'Movie' fleet."

* * * *

When we returned to port we learned of the thrilling raid upon Ostend, in which the "Movies" had played the same vital and plucky part they had in the earlier Zeebrugge raid.

Commodore Herbert Lynes had been entrusted with the planning of the raid, which was to block effectively

the Ostend Harbor, where, for three years, U-boats had a most important base from which to threaten the Allies.

The great difficulty lay in effecting a surprise, when the enemy was already warned by the previous attempts that had failed.

The Germans had removed every mark that showed the channel into the Harbor, and mine fields were everywhere. They had also cut great gaps in the piers to prevent a landing—and about nine German destroyers were lurking outside.

Our old battle-scarred cruiser, "Vindictive," was guided by "Movies" as she groped her uncertain way through the black night toward the Harbor entrance.

Picture the terrific scene: a blue-black sky, faintly sprinkled with stars; scarcely a breath of wind; with the black silhouettes of the British fleet moving stealthily and quietly toward the Ostend Harbor entrance.

The Elco "Movies" were the eyes and ears—all the five senses—to the units of that daring expedition. They showed themselves as flying crests of foam, darting here, there—everywhere, before the advancing fleet.

From the coast of Flanders rose and fell the "Summer lightning" of continual artillery fire; and from over in Dunkirk came a sudden, furious flare of gunfire, telling that German aeroplanes were passing on their way to Calais for a night attack.

The "Vindictive," bearing all her honored Zeebrugge scars, slowly forged through the black waters, intent on her mission.

A timed schedule had been laid down for every step of the attack. The first element of surprise was that there should be no preliminary bombardment of the Harbor and batteries. Smoke barrages were planned for every possible shift of the wind.

Monitors were anchored seaward, awaiting the signal, and the huge sea-batteries of the Royal Marine Artillery in Flanders stood by, waiting to engage the big German Batteries, while aircraft hovered in the background—waiting for the moment when they were to deluge the

She might be a "Hunnish" neutral.

fortifications with their bombs. And everywhere darted the restless "Movies," feeling the way ahead, scouting and carrying orders — thus was the scene set for the great battle of Ostend.

Just fifteen minutes before the "Vindictive" was due at the Harbor entrance—two "Movies" dashed for the ends of the piers and torpedoed them. The eastern end of the pier disappeared in a burst and roar of flame—the signal for our monitors.

Up to that wild moment not a sign of life had come from the Germans. But now a flame rose high in the air and slowly sank. It was the sign from the German aircraft that they had seen and understood.

The "Vindictive" was steadily, ominously gliding ahead, guided and protected by "Movies"—that threw so baffling a smoke screen about her that the beams from enemy searchlights were broken off short.

Then the huge German defense guns roared into action, answered immediately by the equally great guns of the Royal Marine Artillery in Flanders—and Hell was let loose.

German aircraft flew over us, dropping their bombs, and our anti-aircraft guns searched the sky for them. Strings of luminous green balls floated in the air, set loose by our aeroplanes—sending a ghastly green light over the smoke banks, and star shells flared up everywhere.

(Above) M. L.'s throwing out smoke screens.

(Below) M. L.'s guiding "Vindictive" into harbor—and rescuing survivors.

It was then that a thick fog descended, smothering our fleet in complete darkness.

Sirens began to groan as a means of communication, and the Dover flares, with which every "Movie" was equipped, were lighted. And by this dim, clouded light the British Fleet groped its way onward.

As a rift suddenly came in the fog, one of the "Movies" made out the Harbor entrance—and dashed for it, planting a flare on the waters between the piers—and the "Vindictive" steamed over it and on *inside*. The German guns found her at once and machine guns swept her decks—*but she was in*.

Commander Godsal of the "Vindictive" ordered the officers to go with him to the conning tower—and, from that point of vantage, they saw the wrecked pier was breached 200 yards from the seaward end. The "Vindictive" laid her battered nose against the pier and prepared to swing her 320 feet of length across the channel.

A shell killed Commander Godsal and wrecked the conning tower. Lieutenant Crutchley took command. After he had worked the "Vindictive" around as far as possible he gave orders to abandon the ship.

The last engineer to leave the engine room threw the switch that blew the main charges, while from the wreck of the conning tower Crutchley blew the auxiliary charges in the for'ard magazine. The old ship shuddered as the explosives tore the bottom plates and bulkheads from her—and then sank to the bottom of the Channel. Her work was done—the Harbor was blocked.

The "Movies" stood by throughout the entire action and took off the "Vindictive's" crew.

One "Movie," loaded with survivors, raced to the "Warwick," with her cargo safe, but herself in a sinking

condition. As soon as her crew and survivors were safely transferred a demolition charge was placed in her engine room—and she went down to an honored grave.

Such was the raid on Ostend, where the "M.L.'s" played so glorious a part; and had I space I could go on and tell of hundreds of daring exploits performed by these plucky little ships during the Great War.

* * * *

We were convoying a big liner into port when the wonderful news of the Armistice was caught by the wireless.

A great cheering broke from the liner's decks, while the passengers clung to one another, or danced, or walked about in a daze, on her decks.

As for the crew of our little "M. L."—we couldn't quite grasp it, and though in our hearts we believed it—our words were mostly those of disbelief.

It remained for our cook to bring us around. He came up on deck and took it all in. Then he stepped back, looked at the rest of us with an awed solemnity—and said:

"Men—it's orle over."

* * * *

And there ends the brilliant story of the "M.L.'s" in battle on the high seas.

Had it not been for the creation of this fleet of small craft—the "M. L.'s"—the trawlers—and the drifters—the strength of England's Grand Fleet would have been rapidly dispersed and the British Isles would have been open to invasion.

To the men in that American plant, who, by their foresight, energy and experience, proved the value of *standardized* boat building—first with their "M.L.'s," and later by *standardizing* the 5,500-ton fabricated steel cargo ships—will go the highest gratitude of a world set free from the menace of the Hun.

> *"When our last patrol is over*
> *And no more I go to sea,*
> *Then no more I'll be a rover,*
> *No more sailor will I be.*
> *Just a farm set in a valley*
> *Where no U-boats lurk and dwell,*
> *No more hammocks, no more galley,*
> *When I leave this 'Old' M. L."*

NOTE: The Elco Works of Bayonne, N. J., U. S. A., built and delivered a total of 722 Submarine Chasers for the United States and the Allies—more than all the other boat builders of the world combined. It was through this experience that its parent company—the Submarine Boat Corporation—undertook, at its Newark Bay Shipyard, the building of one hundred and fifty 5,500 ton Steel Cargo Ships for the U. S. Government.

www.ingramcontent.com/pod-product-compliance
Lightning Source LLC
Chambersburg PA
CBHW051719040426
42446CB00008B/962